Working for Myself

WITHDRAWN

THE GREEN TEAM

Tana Reiff

American Guidance Service, Inc.
Circle Pines, Minnesota 55014-1796
1-800-328-2560

Working for Myself

Beauty and the Business
Clean as a Whistle
Cooking for a Crowd
Crafting a Business
The Flower Man
Handy All Around
Other People's Pets
You Call, We Haul
Your Kids and Mine

Cover Illustration: James Balkovek
Cover Design: Ina McInnis
Text Designer: Diann Abbott

Printed in the United States of America
ISBN 0-7854-1111-9 (Previously ISBN 1-56103-906-3)
Product Number 40834
A 0 9 8 7 6 5 4 3 2

CONTENTS

Chapter

Grass Tricks

On one side of the fence Tony Ramirez was mowing his family's lawn. On the other side of the fence, Bob Dent was mowing *his* lawn.

Tony was a young man, still in school. He wasn't tall, but he was well-built. Bob was an older man, and a little bigger than Tony. The two men had started mowing at the same time, about 9:00 in the morning. They worked at about the same speed. Yet Tony didn't seem to be feeling the work as much. The sun was beating down hard, but he didn't seem to mind. Bob's shirt was soaked with sweat, and his face was red.

There were other differences, too. Tony's mower was set high. It cut the grass to a height of three inches. Bob's mower was set low. It cut the grass to just over an inch.

Tony pushed the mower in circles toward the middle of the yard. Bob cut his grass in straight lines. He walked back and forth, making sharp turns at the end of each row.

Tony's mower blades ran 24 inches across. His circles took him two miles that morning. Bob's blades were 18 inches across. He walked almost three miles to cut a lawn of the same size.

Tony didn't need to mow close to the trees in his yard. By putting down a circle of mulch around each tree, he saved two feet of mowing. The grass grew right up to Bob's trees. Bob cut in as close as the mower would go. Later he would trim even closer by hand.

Around 10:15, Tony wiped off his mower blades. He sharpened them for the next time. Then he wheeled the mower into the shed and went into the house. He came back out a few minutes later with a glass of iced tea. Then he sat on the backyard deck and enjoyed his cold drink.

Next door Bob was still working. He raked and bagged his clippings. He trimmed around the trees. Then he threw chemical fertilizer all over his lawn. At last he put away his mower. He didn't stop to clean and sharpen the blades.

"How did you finish so fast?" Bob called over to young Tony. "Our lawns are just about the same size. Am I just getting old or what?"

Whenever Tony smiled, his chin turned up and his eyes glowed. He was wearing that special smile now. "I have some tricks!" he said to his neighbor with a smile.

"Like what?" Bob asked.

"Did you notice how I mow in circles instead of rows?" Tony asked. "It's much faster mowing in circles!"

"Well, I did notice that I cut my lawn shorter," said Bob. "But why is your lawn green and mine brown?"

"It's better to cut high," said Tony. "That keeps the sun off the weeds, so they can't grow. And the higher the grass, the deeper the roots. The lawn stays greener through the dry summer months that way."

"But you do have a lot of clover and dandelions," Bob said.

"I don't see them as weeds," said Tony. "Clover is soft and green. Dandelion greens are good to eat!"

"Of course, I fertilize my lawn, too," Bob said. "That takes more time."

"I fertilize, too," said Tony.

"You do not," said Bob. "I would have

seen you if you had."

"Well, you see that I don't pick up the grass clippings," said Tony. "They break down into good fertilizer. And I also put organic fertilizer on the lawn twice a year."

Bob laughed. "They say the grass is always greener on the other side of the fence. That sure is true here!"

"Grass clippings, higher cut, and good, sharp mower blades," Tony said. "Everything adds up."

Looking at his neighbor's lawn made Bob jealous. After all, he worked hard on his lawn, too. But it didn't look nearly as good as Tony's did.

"How does a young guy like you know so much about lawns?" Bob finally asked Tony.

"Well, I just find out what works best and that's what I do," Tony said. "I've learned a lot from my uncle, too. There are all kinds of tricks you can use to have a great lawn."

"You're pretty smart for your age," said Bob. "You even seem to *like* lawn work!"

"It gives me a good feeling," said Tony. "After I'm done, I like to sit back and look at my beautiful lawn. It makes me feel proud."

"I like a nice lawn, too," said Bob. "But I really hate the work. Let me ask you something. How much would you charge to take care of my lawn for me?"

"I don't know," said Tony. "I'll have to think about it."

"Heck, with all you know, you could make yourself a good part-time job out of lawn care," said Bob.

Tony Ramirez smiled again. "Why don't you come over and have a glass of tea with me?"

"I don't mind if I do," said Bob Dent.

For the next half hour, the young man and his older neighbor got to know each other a little better. They talked about baseball for a while, and they talked about cars. But mostly, they talked about lawns.

CHAPTER 2

Improving Lawns

Tony told Bob Dent that he had a "chemical lawn." He called it that because over the years Bob had not let nature do its job. Tony said that adding chemical fertilizer and cutting the grass too low were hard on the lawn. Now it needed help. Tony knew some ways to get the grass back in shape.

First he brought over a flat stick. The stick was marked with a line, two inches from the bottom. Tony put the stick into the ground up to the line. Then he put another mark on the stick, three inches above the ground.

"That's how high we want your grass to be," Tony said to Bob.

"That's pretty high, don't you think?"

"Not as high as it's going to get!" Tony said with a little smile.

Then Tony put a third mark on the stick. This one was an inch above the last one—*four* inches above the ground. "That's how high we'll let the grass grow before we mow," he said.

Next Tony wanted to check the soil for chinch bugs. "Dry grass that gets a little brown is not so bad," he said. "But I don't like these yellow patches. I've got an idea what the problem is."

Tony got an old coffee can with both ends cut out. He stuck the can into Bob's lawn. Then he poured some fresh water from the hose into the can.

"If you have chinch bugs, they'll float

up in about five minutes."

Sure enough, a few tiny black bugs rose to the top of the water. Then a few more came up. Pretty soon there were dozens of chinch bugs floating in the coffee can.

"Big trouble," said Tony. "More than 20 chinch bugs means that you have a problem."

Tony mixed some soap and water together. He sprayed it over Bob's lawn. Then he laid big rags over the wet grass. A whole army of chinch bugs seemed to crawl out of the ground. They stuck like glue to the rags.

After a few minutes Tony rolled the rags into a ball. Then he stuffed the rag ball into Bob's trash can.

"Now we'll see what happens," he said.

"I can't believe you, kid," said Bob, shaking his head. "I'm twice your age and I don't know any of this stuff."

"Well, I've learned a few things over the past few years," said Tony. His special smile was showing once again.

Mrs. Geary called from over the fence. She lived on the other side of Bob Dent's yard. She had been watching both men while they were working on Bob's lawn.

"Tony!" she called. "Will you please come over here when you get time? I need you to take a look at my yard, too."

"Your grass will be ready to mow in about four days," Tony told Bob. "Just keep checking the mark on that stick in the ground."

Tony took the coffee can and another stick over to Mrs. Geary's. He tested her lawn for chinch bugs. It turned out that her lawn also had them. He left a marked stick in the ground to show her just when the lawn should be mowed.

Mrs. Geary could tell that Tony knew what he was doing. She asked him if he would work on her lawn, too. He agreed.

Four days later, Bob Dent's grass was ready to be cut. Tony pushed the mower clockwise around Bob's yard. When he did that, the clippings blew back onto the lawn. The next time around, the clippings got cut again. This time, when the fine bits of grass fell back into the lawn, they hardly showed at all.

After Tony reached the center of the yard, he went back and mowed the edges. When he was finished, the whole lawn was only three inches high.

Bob wasn't sure he liked what he saw. "I'm just not used to such high grass," he said to Tony.

"Come over here," said Tony. "Take off your shoes. Now walk across your lawn and see how it feels."

"It *is* nice," Bob said. "And it feels a whole lot fuller."

"Believe me, you're going to have greener grass," said Tony. "Just you wait and see."

Sure enough, before long Bob's lawn began looking green and healthy.

So did Mrs. Geary's. Tony also noticed that her three flower beds looked like they needed help. In fact, he couldn't keep his eyes off of them. He didn't know much about flowers, just what he had heard from his uncle. But Tony was interested in making Mrs. Geary's whole yard look good. He knew who to talk to.

Tony's uncle had a first name, but no one knew what it was. Everyone called him *Tio*, the Spanish word for uncle. Tio's great love in life was his garden. Even strangers came to see it because they'd heard it was so beautiful. And it was always changing.

Tony went to see his uncle. Tio showed the young man every flower, herb, and vegetable in his garden. He explained that certain flowers bring certain birds and good bugs. And certain birds and good bugs eat certain bad bugs. Tony loved to hear his uncle Tio talk about gardening. With no effort at all his brain soaked up the old man's every word.

That evening Tony went back to Mrs. Geary's house.

"Tio says that daisies and black-eyed Susans bring the big-eyed bug," Tony said. "And you know what? The big-eyed bug eats chinch bugs!"

"I'm very fond of daisies and black-eyed Susans!" she said. "I'll get some at the nursery and put them in right away. I'll miss my herbs, though."

"Don't dig out your herbs," Tony told her. "They bring good bugs, too."

"Well, isn't that something!" said Mrs. Geary. "I'm going to love my yard even more than ever!"

CHAPTER 3

Growing a Business

Bob Dent and Mrs. Geary told their friends about Tony Ramirez.

"He's magic," Mrs. Geary would say to anyone who would listen.

"He knows an awful lot for a young guy," Bob Dent told all the neighbors.

After school Tony went to see other people in the neighborhood about yard care. They all wanted someone to mow for them. They all wanted better-looking lawns. And they all had one other thing in common. They all wanted to stop using chemicals on their lawns.

Tony looked over each neighbor's lawn. Then he told the owner how much he would charge to mow it. Within a few weeks, he was working on lawns nearly every day after school.

Soon people were asking Tony to do other jobs as well. One day he cleared thick brush and trimmed trees and hedges. He did the work, but he didn't like it very much. Even though he wore thick gloves, his arms got scratched up. And he had to rent a truck to haul away the branches and trimmings.

"I want to have my own mulcher someday," Tony said to himself. "Today I could have ground up all those clippings instead of having to haul them away."

At another house, Tony was asked to cut down some small trees. He rented a chain saw. He cut down the trees and then trimmed off the small branches.

Finally he cut up the whole tree for firewood. He stacked the wood in the owner's back yard.

One day a new customer asked Tony to put chemical fertilizer on his lawn. Tony didn't like using chemicals. But he didn't want to lose a new customer, either. "Let me think about it for a while," he said to Mr. Santana.

That night Tio came to Tony's house for dinner. He brought along fresh vegetables from his garden.

In his younger days, Tio had owned a small store where he sold his own vegetables. Now he spent all of his time working in his garden. But he still knew something about running a business.

"Say *no* to the chemicals," Tio said. "Looks to me like you are growing yourself a business, boy. And the first rule of business is to set yourself apart from the others. One way you can do that is by not using chemicals. It's healthier for grass *and* for people without the chemicals."

That sounded right to Tony. "OK, I'll do it your way, Tio," he said.

Tony called the Santanas. He told them he would rather not use chemicals in his business. He said they could easily find someone else who would agree to put chemicals on their lawn.

But the Santanas didn't want someone else. "We hear you are really good with lawns," Mr. Santana said. "We'll give your way a try. If it doesn't work, then we'll call someone else."

"OK, great!" said Tony.

"And can you bring your own mower?" Mr. Santana asked.

Up to now, Tony had not used his family's mower on other lawns. But he liked that mower a lot. He took special care of it. He always kept the blades clean and sharp.

"Sure, I'll bring my mower," he told Mr. Santana. Then he added, "But I will have to charge extra."

After Tony hung up the phone, he thought of something else. How in the world was he going to get the mower to the Santana house? He began to wish he hadn't agreed so quickly.

"Hey, Dad, can I take our lawn mower to a job tomorrow after school?" Tony asked his father.

"You want to take *our* lawn mower?" said Mr. Ramirez. "How are you going to get it to your customer's house?"

"I have to figure out a way to tow it," Tony said.

"Well, even so, I'm not sure I want you using our mower on your jobs. That will add a lot of extra wear and tear on it. If it breaks down, will you be able to pay for the repairs?"

Mr. Ramirez saw the disappointed look on Tony's face. "Tell you what," he said. "You may use our mower for two months. After that you should buy your own mower with the money you make."

"That's fair," said Tony.

Tony spent that evening building a flat trailer. He laid boards across two-by-fours. He hammered a floor and sides together. He attached wheels. Then he built a ramp to load the mower onto the trailer. Finally he hitched the trailer to the rear bumper of the family car with a tow bar.

It rained the next day. Tony was glad to see rain. His lawns needed water badly. But the weather stayed gray and cool. Long after the rain stopped, the grass was still wet. Even so, Tony towed the family mower to the Santana house.

It was a big lawn. The mower didn't like the wet grass. Tony had to stop again and again to pull grass out of the blades. Cutting wet grass wasn't really good for the lawn, either. Still, Tony managed to get the job done.

Tony looked at the check he received from the Santanas. "This check will not go to buy clothes," he told himself. "This check will not be used to buy even a plain, old lawn mower." The trouble Tony had mowing the Santanas' wet lawn told him something. The message was that he needed a bigger, stronger mower. He tucked the check into his jacket pocket.

The next day Tony took the check to the bank. He opened a savings account so he could put away money to buy a mower that meant business.

CHAPTER 4

Summer Heat

By the time the school year ended, Tony had plenty of lawn care jobs lined up for the summer.

He couldn't have found better work for the summer. The year before, he had worked at a fast food restaurant. Two years ago he couldn't find a job at all. Now he wondered why he hadn't thought of lawn care before. It was hard work at times, but it was work that he enjoyed more than anything else in the world.

Tony walked to many of his jobs. One day he walked four blocks to get to a job. Then he walked four blocks home. Then he walked five blocks in the other direction. Then he walked eight blocks to a job that was only one block away from the first job.

"Wait a minute!" Tony said to himself. "Why am I walking up and down the same street two times in the same day? It doesn't make sense."

He thought about his car trips, too. He borrowed the family car to drive to jobs in the Brookside neighborhood on Monday and Tuesday. Why couldn't he do both Brookside jobs on the same day? Now he had the whole summer to work. He knew he could come up with a schedule that would make better use of his time.

That night Tony sat down with a calendar. He made a list of all the lawns he had to do that week. He wrote all the

Brookside jobs on the calendar under Monday. He wrote all the east side jobs for Tuesday. He listed all the west side jobs under Wednesday.

He tried the new plan right away. The first week he saved so much time he couldn't believe it. The next Monday he was able to fit in an extra Brookside job. The extra money meant extra savings.

It was a great plan.

Then the summer weather became very dry. The grass stopped growing so fast. On his Brookside day, Tony found the lawns there were too short to cut. They would be ready by Friday—but that was his Oak Hill day. The Oak Hill jobs wouldn't be ready to cut until the following Tuesday.

Tony was upset. His schedule was a mess! But he used his head. First he called all his Brookside customers. "How does your lawn look today?" he asked Mr. Simmons.

"It doesn't seem to need cutting today,"

Mr. Simmons said.

"I'll put you down for Friday, OK?" Tony asked.

He moved all his Brookside jobs to Friday. Then he moved *all* his jobs up by three days. He made sure to keep all of each day's jobs together. The plan worked.

At the end of each job Tony got paid. The next morning he would take all of the checks to the bank. Part of every check went into his savings account toward the new mower.

He had a new job in Southgate one day. "I'm lucky," Tony said to himself as he pushed the mower around the Bennetts' lawn. "I never have to wait for my money. Everybody always pays me right away."

When he finished the lawn, he went to the door to pick up his check from Mrs. Bennett.

"I'm sorry," she said. "I won't be able to pay you today. Can you come back tomorrow?"

The next day Tony would be working in Oak Hill. Coming back to Southgate would be out of his way.

"I won't be in the neighborhood tomorrow," said Tony. "Why don't you mail me the check?"

"Sure," said Mrs. Bennett. "I'll do that." So Tony wrote down his address and gave it to Mrs. Bennett.

Tony opened up the mailbox on Saturday. There was no check from the Bennetts. It didn't come on Monday, Tuesday, or Wednesday, either.

Thursday was the Bennetts' mowing day. Tony went to their house and knocked on the door. No one was home.

He didn't know what to do. The Bennetts' lawn was high enough to cut. But Mrs. Bennett still hadn't paid him yet for the week before.

He wrote a note. "Sorry. Could not mow your lawn. Must pay for last week first. Please call."

Tony never heard from the Bennetts

again. Later one of the neighbors told him that the Bennetts had gone away for the rest of the summer.

From that day on, Tony asked new customers to pay up front for the first few times. Some people didn't want to do that. But Tony made it a rule. By now he had plenty of customers—more than he could handle.

CHAPTER 5

Taking the Leap

Tony was doing great things with his customers' lawns. But wet grass was always a problem. And if the grass was too tall, the mower missed a patch here and there. Then Tony had to run over the whole lawn a second time. He knew he needed a bigger mower.

And it couldn't be just *any* big mower. It had to be heavy duty. And it had to be a mower that you could ride on.

One rainy day Tony went to a lawn and garden store. It had a showroom full of heavy-duty riding mowers. As Tony walked through the big glass doors, his eyes went straight to one mower. It was big, and it was painted bright red. "I'll feel like a farmer on his tractor," Tony said to himself.

He put his hand on the mower's front fender. It was shiny, but it felt like a rock. He kicked the tires. They're built to last, he thought to himself. The mower even had headlights, so he could work in the dark if he had to.

"May I help you, sir?" a man's deep voice said.

"Uh, yes . . . yes, you may," Tony began. "This mower here looks pretty good. I run a little lawn-care business. I'm looking for a mower that will do a good job on all kinds of lawns."

"Then this is your machine!" said the salesman with a smile.

He went on to tell Tony all about the

big mower. The powerful engine could get the mower through the tallest grass. The big tires could grip the steepest hills. This machine could do anything. And the body had a ten-year warranty against rust.

"It sounds like just what I need," said Tony. Then he asked the question he had been putting off. "And what's the price?"

The salesperson told him the price. Tony wasn't sure he had heard right, so he asked again. He *had* heard right! The number nearly knocked Tony off his feet.

"Thank you very much," he said in a low voice. "But that's out of the question."

So the salesman quickly showed Tony two other mowers.

The first model he pointed out had a much smaller engine, no lights, and no rust warranty. The body was blue.

The other model had a smaller engine, but it wasn't *too* small. It had lights. It had a five-year rust warranty on the body. And it was red. Tony couldn't explain it. But there was something about that color that he really liked.

Tony thought that this model would be fine. But it still cost a lot of money.

"Maybe we can work something out," said the salesperson. "We have a special program for small businesses like yours. How about if we finance that machine over three years?" He took Tony into his office and worked out the numbers.

Tony would be paying the store quite a bit of money each month. Their interest rates for a three-year loan were very high. He *might* be able to manage it— but it would be tight. He wondered if this finance plan was the best he could find.

"Let me think about it for a few days," Tony told the salesman.

Tony went straight to his bank. He sat down with a loan officer. He found out that the bank could finance the mower for a lot less money. The only difference was that he would have to pay $1,000 as a down payment.

"I'll have to think about it," Tony told the loan officer as he left the bank.

Tony went home to think. He knew how much money he had already put away. He knew how much more he would need to make the down payment. In time he could come up with $1,000. But it would take him another two months. He was already saving a big part of what he made. Putting away even more money would leave him very little to spend on other things.

Tony went to the person he usually went to for advice—Tio.

As always, Tio was working in his garden. "Every business needs its tools," he said. "It takes money just to get a new business going. Some people don't see this when they're just starting out. A new business may not make any money for a long time. You have to *spend* some money to *make* some money."

"It's lucky that I live with my parents," Tony said. "I don't need very much to get by. But I want to have my own place someday. I want to get married. I want to make a good living. I like my work—but I want to make money at it!"

"Sure you do," said his uncle. "But first you must decide something. Will you stay with this business long enough to make money at it? And how long can you get by before your business *has* to make some money?"

"I'll think some more," said Tony.

The next day was sunny. Tony had a lot of lawns to catch up on. He had time to think as he pushed the mower around in circles. All day he added up numbers in his head. He thought about how important this business was to him.

By that evening Tony had made up his mind. For the next few weeks he'd cut down his spending. He'd save every penny he could toward a down payment on the new mower. After that he'd stick to his tight budget. He knew he would *have to* if he was going to make monthly payments on the mower.

Tony had decided to turn his lawn care work into a serious business. It was a big step. But he was ready.

In his mind, Tony could see himself riding his new mower. In his mind, he was riding fast. He was cutting more grass than he could ever cut with a push mower. In his mind, he was almost flying.

Big Joe

The big new mower fit on the trailer perfectly. And there was enough room for the push mower besides. Tony still needed the smaller mower for trimming around trees and brush.

Tony named the new machine Big Joe. He felt like the king of the hill as he rode it on all his jobs that day.

"Nice mower!" cried out Mr. Santana from his kitchen window. Everyone said that the first time they saw Big Joe. Tony had to charge his customers a little more now, but mowing the lawns was taking less time. Most people ended up paying about the same as before.

Tony bought a big gas tank. He bought oil in 55-gallon drums. He bought cases of hydraulic oil and grease. He kept everything in a garage that he rented for a small monthly fee. Tony stopped there once a day to fill up Big Joe's tank with gas and oil. Every now and then he greased Big Joe's engine and changed the oil. Taking care of Big Joe was almost as much fun as riding him.

The days hurried by. Almost overnight it seemed that it wasn't summer anymore. The weather turned cooler. The grass grew more slowly. Instead of once a week, many lawns needed cutting only every other week now. Some shady lawns needed cutting only every three weeks or so.

Soon the money wasn't adding up as

fast as before. Tony had known that fall was coming—but he hadn't really planned for it. Now he was beginning to worry about how he would make the next payment on Big Joe.

"Find another way to make money," Tio told him. "You like lawns. Fine. But, *think*, Tony. What else does a lawn need besides mowing?"

"The leaves are starting to fall," Tony said. "Up to now, falling leaves haven't been a problem. I've just been mulching them in with the grass clippings."

"You watch," said Tio. "The leaves will start to come faster. You can't mulch them all in. Some leaves will have to be raked. There's money in raking."

"And fall is the best time to fertilize around here," Tony said. "I know! I'll line up all my customers and offer them a special deal to fertilize their lawns."

"Fall is a busy time for a lawn!" said Tio. His eyes twinkled. "Just you think some more, Tony!"

"Top dressing!" said Tony. "How could I forget top dressing? It helps thin out the thatch on a lawn."

"Now you're thinking!" said Tio. "Go on. Get out there and line up your work for the fall!"

Tony telephoned every customer he had. Almost all of them wanted him to fertilize their lawns. Leaving the grass clippings was good for the soil, he told everyone. But clippings only feed a lawn about half of what it needs, he explained. The rest must come from fertilizers. But there was still no need for chemicals, Tony said.

So Tony bought pounds of bloodmeal and dried manure. He carried the fertilizer in trash cans on the trailer. The next few weeks he was kept very busy spreading fertilizer on lawns. Some people thought the manure would smell bad, but it didn't.

Bob Dent was worried about thatch. He didn't like that thick layer of dead twigs and leaves building up under his grass. "Maybe too many clippings were left on the lawn," he said.

"People often think clippings cause thatch," Tony explained. "But they don't. One thing that helps is to have plenty of earthworms in your soil. They'll take care of the thatch. Too many years of chemical fertilizers have killed off your earthworms."

Tony said there were two things to do for thatch. First he top-dressed Bob's lawn with a thin layer of soil. Then he used a special tool to poke holes in the soil. That let in air for earthworms.

Over the next two months the leaves fell off the trees like rain from the sky. Tony could hardly keep up with the raking. If he hadn't worn big thick gloves, the rake handle would have worn the skin off his hands.

What to do with all the raked leaves was another problem. In some places, the garbage service picked up leaves along the street. But all neighborhoods didn't have that service. Tony talked those customers into starting a compost heap. By the following year, he said, the leaves would be broken down into rich compost. Then people could dig that compost into their garden soil.

So fall turned out to be a busy season after all. Then the days started getting shorter. The leaves stopped falling. Before long, the trees became bare. And the weather was always cool.

Fertilizing, top dressing, and raking were finished for the year. It was time for Tony and Big Joe to make their last rounds. For the last mow of the season, Tony and Big Joe cut everyone's grass nice and low.

When that was finished, Tony got Big Joe ready for winter. He drained all the gas out of the tank. He pulled out the sparkplug. He sprayed oil inside. He torqued the engine a few times and put the sparkplug back in.

Then Tony wheeled Big Joe into the garage. He patted Big Joe's fender, covered him up, and said good-bye to his friend for the winter.

CHAPTER 7

Winter Work

"Now what do I do?" Tony asked Tio.

Tio was busy digging up flower bulbs. "You're a smart young man," Tio said. "It's winter. That means it's time to think again!"

"I'm thinking," Tony said. "But so far I haven't had any great ideas."

All of a sudden, Tio stood up. "I think I smell smoke!" he said, his nose sniffing at the cool air.

"Is something on fire?" Tony asked.

"Take a deep breath!" Tio told him.

"All I smell is burning wood," Tony said. "Your neighbor must have built a nice fire in his fireplace."

"There you go!" said Tio. "And what do people need so they can get a nice big fire going?"

"Wood, of course," said Tony.

"And where do they *get* that firewood?"

Tony laughed. "I guess I need a chain saw," he said, catching on to Tio's hints at last.

Luckily, Tony had saved enough money to buy one. He didn't need to take out another loan.

In no time at all, Tony was in the firewood business. He put a little ad in the local paper. When someone had a tree to cut down, Tony did it for nothing and kept the wood. If the people wanted to keep the wood, he charged them to cut down the tree. Some people sold him wood, which he then had to saw.

There were a few problems, though. The wood from a freshly cut tree was "green." Tony couldn't sell green wood. If it was wet, it didn't burn well. Wood took time to "cure," or dry out. Tony could sell only seasoned wood or wood cut from trees that were already on the ground.

Then he found out he could cut wood from state land. All he had to do was buy a license. And he learned that he could haul away the leftover wood from a mill for next to nothing.

Tony tied up wood in bundles and stored it behind his garage. Then he loaded cords of wood onto his trailer and took them to his customers.

First Tony called on all his lawn customers who had fireplaces. Then he put up signs to get some new business. He kept a list of everyone who bought wood from him. He would contact those people next year.

Selling firewood kept Tony busy all fall and into the winter. But things slowed down again when the weather got really cold. Then the first big snow came Tony was surprised when his lawn customers began to call.

"We have a driveway full of snow," said Mr. Santana. "Do you have a plow on your tractor?"

"Gee, no," said Tony. "I wish I could help you out. Sorry."

A *snow plow*. "What a great idea!" Tony thought to himself. But then he thought again. "Forget it!" he told himself. "That would cost a lot more money than I've got right now."

The snow plow idea wouldn't leave his mind, though. Tony and his father hand-shoveled their own driveway. It took the two of them a whole hour of hard work. All Tony could think about was how easy the job would have been with a power snow plow.

"Forget it," he told himself again. "Big Joe has been put to bed for the winter. And there isn't any money for a plow—

not this year, anyway."

Then Bob Dent asked Tony to shovel his driveway, too. That job took Tony two hours to do by himself. He couldn't charge Bob enough to make it worth his time. It was very hard work.

Snow plow. Snow plow. It was all that Tony could think about.

When he finished Bob Dent's driveway, Tony went inside and called the lawn and garden store. He found out how much a plow for Big Joe would cost. It was less than he expected.

Next Tony called his loan officer at the bank. "How much more of a loan could I get?" he asked.

The loan officer checked Tony's records. "You haven't missed a payment," he said. "We could probably give you enough for a snow plow. Can you get in here to sign the papers?"

Tony was on the road in a minute. But even the roads that had been plowed were still very bad. Tony drove much faster than he should have.

"How did you get here so fast?" said the loan officer.

"It took me too long to shovel two driveways," said Tony. "I decided to speed up my life a little!"

"The snow drifts are keeping a lot of people home," said the loan officer. "This is a slow day for the bank. Lucky for you, I could move these papers right through. You're not moving *too* fast here, are you, Tony?"

"No, I don't think so," said Tony. "Getting this snow plow can put me in business all year round."

"You'd better hope for a *lot* of snow!" laughed the loan officer. He handed Tony the check for the loan.

When he got home, Tony called the lawn and garden store. He asked them to deliver the snow plow to the garage he rented. He would meet them there.

That night a big new snowstorm blew into town. The temperature was going

down, and the snow drifts were piling up.
Tony had a big smile on his face as he
looked out the window. *Let it snow*, he
said to himself.

The next day Big Joe was on the job
again. Tony was busy again. And the
money was rolling in again.

CHAPTER 8

The Green Team

The first bulb flowers were pushing through the spring soil. And the grass was growing again. As soon as a lawn got two inches high, Tony and Big Joe did the first mow of the season. Cutting off the brown tips early let more sun in. That gave Tony's lawns a strong start.

For the first mow, however, Tony had to rake the grass clippings. Then he didn't mow the lawns again until the grass was looking good and green.

When spring came, Tony heard something new from his customers. Many of them asked him to help them get their gardens started.

The hard soil needed a tilling. Tony knew that from Tio. The first thing every spring Tio turned over his garden soil. After that he would wait a week until the weeds got started. Then he would till the young shoots back into the soil.

Tony's customers also wanted to know how to keep bugs away. They wanted to know which flowers and herbs to choose. They wanted to know what to plant next to the vegetables. They had a lot of questions—and Tony knew only a few of the answers.

He went to Tio, of course. Tio had a tiller that Tony could borrow. And Tio knew all there was to know about gardening without chemicals.

When Tony arrived, Tio was hard at work in his back yard. "I love the dirt under my nails!" he said. "It makes me feel alive. Look at this, Tony! I'm putting in a butterfly garden this year."

"Your gardens always look so beautiful," Tony told his uncle. "How do you do it, Tio?"

"I have an eye," was all Tio said.

"Well, I need your eye," said Tony. "Everyone's asking me to plan gardens for them. The truth is that I don't know how. Will you help me?"

"I'm pretty busy with my own garden," said Tio.

"I can see that," said Tony. "Maybe I better stick to lawns." He kicked a rock as he spoke. Tio could see that Tony was disappointed.

"All right," Tio said. "I'll plan just one garden for you. Go ahead and pick your favorite customer."

"That's great!" Tony said. "I really appreciate it."

Tony picked Mrs. Geary. Tio came to look at her yard. He told her to keep most of the plants she already had. Then Tio drew a plan for improving Mrs. Geary's garden. He knew the names of each and every plant.

"That was too easy," he told Tony later. "Let me do another one."

So Tio went to see the Santanas. Their yard was much bigger than Mrs. Geary's. And they were starting with nothing.

Tony watched closely as Tio drew the Santanas' garden plan. He couldn't believe how fast his old uncle worked. Tio seemed to pull everything right out of his head. He never even opened a book.

That evening, Tony sat with Tio on his back yard patio. "I've been thinking, Tio," Tony said. "I'd like you to go into business with me. We could call ourselves Lawn and Garden. I'm Lawn—you're Garden. What do you say?"

"These are supposed to be my golden years!" Tio said, laughing. "Why would I want to start out in business all over again with a sprout like you?"

"Because you'd be great," said Tony. "The two of us working together would make a great team."

Tio didn't speak for a few minutes. Tony was hoping he would just say, "Sure, I'll go into business with you." But Tio was quiet.

"What are you thinking, Tio?" Tony asked at last.

"I'm thinking about a deal," Tio said. "I've really enjoyed working out these garden plans. I can't remember when I ever had so much fun except in my own garden. I'm just not so sure that I want to get tied into a new business—at my age, you know."

"I can understand that," Tony said. "So what's the deal?"

"How about if I help you out," Tio asked. "I'll *plan* the gardens. But you will have to do the hard work. You know— like the digging and planting."

"Great!" said Tony.

"First you must learn more about

gardens," Tio went on. "One thing you can do is to watch me work. But you also need to sign up for a class. You need to become a master gardener."

"OK!" Tony said.

"And we need a better name than just Lawn and Garden," said Tio. "How about the Green Team? It catches the ear better!"

"It's a deal!" said Tony.

With that, Tony ran right out and had some new business cards printed up. They said:

THE GREEN TEAM

The Best Care for Your

Lawn and Garden

To Tony, the business now seemed complete. He felt that he and Tio could do anything. Together they could mow grass, clear brush, rake leaves, cut wood, and plow snow. They could plan gardens and take care of them, too. The business could run all year round.

Tony knew he would enjoy riding

around with Tio, listening to his stories. And together they might get new business. Tony had been thinking about taking care of the grounds around office buildings. But something even better was yet to come.

CHAPTER 9

Master Gardeners

The master gardener class started the following Monday night. Tony and Tio had a lot of work lined up for that week. Tony almost wished he hadn't signed up for the class. But he knew it was part of his agreement with Tio, so he made sure to get there.

Tony arrived at the class a few minutes early. The walls of the room were lined with pictures of beautiful gardens. There were all kinds of flower gardens and vegetable gardens. Every one of them was full of color. Every garden had a beautiful lawn around it. Tony looked at the pictures with his mouth wide open. He wished he could make his customers' lawns and gardens look just like the pictures.

Then he spotted something even more beautiful than the gardens. A young woman had walked into the classroom. She was short, just a little shorter than Tony. She had long, dark hair and large brown eyes. She was like no one Tony had ever seen before. He could tell from her eyes that she had a sharp mind.

Tony didn't talk to the young woman that night. But he thought about her all week. He saw her face in every flower he planted. Even a shiny blade of grass made Tony think of her long, shiny hair.

So the next Monday, he got up his courage and walked over to her. "Hi, my name is Tony," he said.

"What?" the young woman said.

"I said my name is Tony. Tony Ramirez."

"I thought I was hearing things," the young woman said. "*My* name is Toni, too. With an *i*."

They both laughed.

The class worked in teams that night. Each team of three students had to plan an herb garden. Tony and Toni worked on the same team. After class, Tony and Toni talked for more than an hour.

The following Monday the class met at a real garden. The students looked at the soil and talked about what it needed. Then the class was divided into the same teams as the week before. Only this time the third person on Tony and Toni's team was not there. Tonight it was just the two of them.

"I say this soil needs a deep bed of stones first," said Toni. "It should be dug three feet down. A bed of stones will give water a place to go."

"Right," said Tony.

"After that, the soil will need about 50 pounds of manure," said Toni.

"Why do you say 50?" Tony asked the pretty young woman.

"Remember what the teacher said? One pound of manure for every three square feet of soil," said Toni.

"Right."

"And then . . ." Toni went on.

"Wait a minute!" said Tony. "It's my turn! I say this soil should get about five pounds of bone meal."

Toni wrote everything down.

Next they talked about which flowers to plant in which parts of the garden.

When they were finished, Tony said, "I could talk with you for hours, Toni. You make planning a garden seem like the most interesting thing in the world."

They went out after class that night to talk some more. And the next week. And the next. Then they started going out on Saturday nights and on week nights in between classes.

"You're going to have to meet my uncle sometime," Tony said one Saturday night. He told Toni about Tio's garden.

But she had already heard about Tio's garden. Nearly everyone in town had heard about Tio's garden. Toni said she had wanted to see it for years. She couldn't believe that the famous Tio was really Tony's uncle.

The next day the two of them went to visit Tio. As always, Tio was happy to see Tony. And he took to Toni right away. Tio had always treated Tony like a son. He treated Toni almost like a daughter from the minute he met her.

Toni wanted to learn everything about Tio's garden. Tio showed her his bellflowers and daisies and lilies. And the roses! Tio had won many prizes for his wonderful roses.

"You should marry this young woman!" Tio told Tony.

Toni put her head down and laughed

a little. She couldn't look Tony in the eye.

"Marry her?" said Tony. He was smiling. His eyes glowed. "That's a very good idea, Tio. What do you say, Toni? I love you very much. Will you marry me?"

Right then and there, in Tio's garden, Toni and Tony decided to get married.

"Don't stop there," Tio said. "Now let's ask this smart young woman to join the family business."

Tony had thought about marrying Toni long before Tio said anything. But he hadn't thought about asking her to join the business.

"I'll think about it," said Tony. But after only a few seconds he had thought about it long enough. "You're right, Tio. Of course she should join the business! How about it, Toni? Would you like to be our partner?"

Tony and Toni graduated as master gardeners in May. They were married in Tio's garden in June. The roses were in full bloom.

The business took on a whole new life with Toni in it. Like her husband, she was full of ideas. Like Tio, she had a good eye. She was always ready to learn something new. And right from the beginning she worked very hard.

Toni was the best thing that ever happened to Tony Ramirez.

C H A P T E R   10

Fruits of Labor

Three years later . . .

Tony did most of his thinking while riding Big Joe. Somehow the fun of riding that big machine never wore off. Every day with Big Joe was a pleasure to Tony.

Today Tony was thinking about how much his life had changed. Only three years ago he was a boy just out of high school. He was living at home. He was mowing lawns for a little extra money.

Now he was a married man and a father. Baby Edward was almost a year old. Big Joe was paid off. Tony and his wife Toni were making good money running a full-time, year-round business. They lived with Toni's family in a big place on the edge of town. The house was surrounded by a huge yard.

Having all that ground was good for the business, too. Big Joe could stay in an old barn near the road. Toni could sell firewood at a roadside stand. And finally, Tony was able to buy a mulcher. Never again would he have to haul away extra grass clippings, branches, or trimmings. Instead, he loaded them up in his new truck and brought them home. Then he threw them on a compost heap. He saved hundreds of dollars by using his own compost to improve his customers' lawns and gardens.

Tony and Toni didn't have much free time. What little time they had they spent with Edward and working on their own grounds. They had turned much of their property into beautiful flower, herb, and vegetable gardens.

Tio was proud of the young couple. After all, he had taught them both a lot. Toni did most of the garden plans now. Tio slowly backed away from the family business. He wasn't as strong as he used to be. He wanted to put all his energy into his own garden again.

One spring day Tony's old neighbor Bob Dent called. "Sign me up for lawn care again this year," he said. "Mrs. Geary wants you to do hers, too."

"Well, I have to tell you—our prices are going up a little this year," Tony said.

"No problem," said Bob. "I couldn't find a better gardener than you."

Toni came along when Tony went to see the old neighbors. Tony's parents had moved away. So he hadn't been back to his old neighborhood for quite a while.

Tony mowed while his wife took care of Mrs. Geary's garden. By the time they finished, they were hot and thirsty.

"Everybody come over and have a glass of iced tea," Bob Dent said.

The four of them sat on Bob's deck and had a cold drink together. To Tony, it felt like old times—only different. So much had changed.

"I forgot to tell you something," Tony said to Bob and Mrs. Geary. "We're running a special right now. My first two customers of the season get a free lawn service. Those two customers happen to be you and Mrs. Geary. What do you think of that?"

"You always were a smart young man," Bob Dent said. "Good at lawns and good at business. You know how to keep your customers happy!"

A few miles away, Tio's hands were deep in his garden. There was dirt under his nails. A band of butterflies fluttered over his head. Tio felt young and alive. This was just the way he liked his days to be.